CONCEPTS

"Where Motivation Stems from Within"

Monique Chandler Walker, MBA

Book Cover Design: Lock It! Graphics

© Copyright 2005 Monique Chandler Walker

Ultimate NRG Journal

ISBN: 0-9763698-8-5

Thank You....

Mom and Dad,

Thank you for allowing me to grow and become who I am today. My happiness and enthusiasm stems from the love and support of my family. Dad, I sincerely thank you for standing your ground and showing me the way. Mom, I sincerely thank you for always waking up in the middle of the night when I just wanted to chat. Mom and Dad, I appreciate both of you for always smiling before you pick up the phone to talk to me. I thank you so much for teaching me how to love people and respect them for who they are. I'm so delighted to have parents that are my #1 fans.

"Just be nice, let God fight your battles."
-Mom

Granny Chandler,

Thank you for always believing in all of the family and for not having a favorite. You are the Queen of our family and we are so grateful to have you as our granny. I know granddad is looking down on us with a joyful smile because of how close we are. We love you so much.

And...

To those who dislike me for whatever reason, I thank you for motivating me through your negative energy. It was through your negative energy that I learned how to deal with challenging personalities. Again, THANK YOU! Just a thought for you, it takes absolutely no energy to be nice.

Acknowledgements....

Rena Morgan – I am forever grateful to have you as a spiritual sounding board. Your love, kindness and thoughtfulness has meant so much to me. My Mom and I appreciate all the support that you have unselfishly given through the years.

Debbie Phillips – Your enthusiasm is contagious and has been very motivating in my life.

Imani Price- Abdelrazzaq and Donna Hunter – I feel privileged to have two best friends that are strong-willed, creative, honest, nuturing, and energetic.

Kimberly B. Carreker – I am grateful for your caring and support in whatever I decided to do.

Rev. Marjorie Hale – I am grateful because you taught me how to become the person I dreamed of becoming

Dr. Jean DeVard-Kemp – I am grateful because you taught me the old school rules and how to ask for what I want.

Angela Harrington Rice – I am grateful because you taught me how to find my inner girl.

Robin DeMorse, Brenda Little and Wendy Arce – I am grateful for your encouragement in knowing that I could make this dream a reality.

Tracy Bowers and Kari Campbell – Thank you for the many challenging opportunities and for believing that I could make a difference.

"Let us evaluate our strengths, for it is in our uniqueness that defines our true identity."

Debbie Phillips, The Quadrillion
Stockbridge, GA

"Put yourself in the position
to do the choosing
instead of waiting to be chosen."

Carolyn Peck
Head Women's Basketball Coach
University of Florida

'u' make it a GREAT day!

"Embrace Your Life!"

'u' make it a GREAT day!

"You are a Shining Super Star!"

'u' make it a GREAT day!

"Are you interested or are you committed? There is a difference. Are you interested in your success or are you committed to your success? Find the commitment, or soon your interest will move on to something else."

Dawn Gartin
Creative Memories
Unit Leader and Business Trainer

'u' make it a GREAT day!

_____

_____

_____

_____

_____

_____

_____

_____

_____

_____

_____

_____

_____

_____

_____

"I am awesome and I like myself more and more each day."

'u' make it a GREAT day!

"When you are seeking to do your very best, always remember the inner you."

Tammy Jackson, Retired
Houston Comets-WNBA

'u' make it a GREAT day!

"You are special to so many people."

'u' make it a GREAT day!

"There is enough pie for all of us to have one.... why settle for a slice."

'u' make it a GREAT day!

"Become the person you dreamed of becoming and not the person society says you should become."

'u' make it a GREAT day!

_____

_____

_____

_____

_____

_____

_____

_____

_____

_____

_____

_____

_____

_____

_____

_____

"Love is an action word, it is not always what one says, but rather what one does to show that love."

Janice Davis Mortimer
Executive Assistant to the Secretary
Florida Department of Corrections

'u' make it a GREAT day!

"Stay focused on your goals."

'u' make it a GREAT day!

"Believe in yourself every day."

'u' make it a GREAT day!

"When I think about the power of the mirror, I truly believe that you become what you see and I hope one day some young women would want to be like me."

Carolyn Peck
Head Women's Basketball Coach
University of Florida

'u' make it a GREAT day!

"Your fan club starts with your family and friends....Enjoy your fan club."

'u' make it a GREAT day!

_____

_____

_____

_____

_____

_____

_____

_____

_____

_____

_____

_____

_____

_____

_____

_____

"Have you learned anything from your mistakes?"

'u' make it a GREAT day!

"Life goes on with or without you...
stay in the race."

'u' make it a GREAT day!

"Obstacles are only as big as you make them. Once you overcome them it makes you wiser and stronger, thus equipping you for the journey that others dare not travel."

-Sylvia Crawley-CEO
Ephod Customs
Durham, NC

'u' make it a GREAT day!

"What positive impact are you making on society?"

'u' make it a GREAT day!

"What are you doing to help others become the best that they can be?"

'u' make it a GREAT day!

"There is nothing like a mother's love. A mother's love is the closest thing to God's love for us. It is our introduction to God, for you know he is love."

Carolyn Brown Spooner
Mayor of Starke

'u' make it a GREAT day!

_____

_____

_____

_____

_____

_____

_____

_____

_____

_____

_____

_____

_____

_____

_____

_____

_____

"Are you happy when you look in the mirror at yourself?"

'u' make it a GREAT day!

"Treat others like you want them to treat your children."

'u' make it a GREAT day!

"Whatever it takes... make it happen... just as quick as you can."

'u' make it a GREAT day!

"You never **use** people....
You **make use** of them."

Bernell Hooker, Founder & CEO
Images of Us Sports
Milwaukee, WI

'u' make it a GREAT day!

"You will be held accountable for the choices you choose to make."

'u' make it a GREAT day!

"Make good sound decisions throughout your life."

'u' make it a GREAT day!

"Knowing who I am as a woman elevates the quality of my life, mind, body, and soul. For I am transformed by the renewing of my **mind**, because I am part of the **body** of Christ. Therefore, my **soul** will never be compromised while dancing to the beat of **life**'s drum."

Laphelia Doss
Assistant Women's Basketball Coach
Eastern Kentucky University

'u' make it a GREAT day!

"Believe in your dreams and follow them through."

'u' make it a GREAT day!

"Today, I will design my lifestyle for tomorrow."

'u' make it a GREAT day!

"This thing called life...I got it now!"

'u' make it a GREAT day!

"The only obstacles that can stop us are the ones that we allow."

Carolyn Peck
Head Women's Basketball Coach
University of Florida

'u' make it a GREAT day!

"You must love yourself first
before you can love someone else."

'u' make it a GREAT day!

"Don't sprint through life
rather live it like a marathon."

'u' make it a GREAT day!

" Pretty is..... as Pretty does."

Donna Hartley
Assistant Principal
Bradford High School

'u' make it a GREAT day!

"Be grateful to see another BIRTHDAY...
Embrace your special day and throw your
own celebration."

'u' make it a GREAT day!

"Nothing worth while is the result of the present. Allow today's desire for success drive you to put forth for tomorrow's fruits. When the seeds of tomorrow blossom, let them be a reminder of yesterday. As for today, be patient, believe, do your best, and know you have invested in tomorrow."

Jannon Roland
Assistant Women's Basketball Coach
Purdue University

'u' make it a GREAT day!

"Get up earlier each day and focus on you... start your day with meditation."

'u' make it a GREAT day!

"You get what you expect and except.
Expect the very best and
accept nothing less."

Carolyn Peck
Head Women's Basketball Coach
University of Florida

'u' make it a GREAT day!

"Life is Good. So keep your chin up!"

'u' make it a GREAT day!

"Success is not based on how wealthy you are or how many championships you win, but on how many lives you touch."

Renà Faust - Holden
Assistant Women's Basketball Coach
University of Arkansas

'u' make it a GREAT day!

"Become your best you...."

'u' make it a GREAT day!

"Expect success, expect greatness!"

Valerie Linley
Assistant Women's Basketball Coach
College of Charleston

'u' make it a GREAT day!

"There is no victory without opposition."

I was thinking about what the Lord meant in I Samuel 15:22, when He said "obedience is better than sacrifice." "Does the Lord delight in burnt offerings and sacrifices as much as in obeying the voice of the Lord?"

I would rather obey God than sacrifice my relationship with him for some temporary thrill or moment of disobedience. It's not always easy to be obedient but man it's so much better than having to confess and ask for forgiveness, when you should have just done the right thing in the first place. Some lessons are harder to learn than others, but I am so thankful that God is slow to anger and abounding in love. Think about that the next time you choose pleasure over obedience, it's not worth the sacrifice.

Fleceia Comeaux
Area Director
South Houston Fellowship of Christian Athletes

'u' make it a GREAT day!

"Have you found your purpose in life?"

Meet Monique.....

"I truly feel that it doesn't matter where you come from. You can be anyone you choose to be. We are all CEOs of our own lives."

-Monique Chandler Walker, MBA

Even before meeting Monique Chandler Walker in person, it is evident that this is a woman who possesses a unique blend of contagious, high-volume, motivational energy. This energy is so pervasive that one need only call her business phone and listen to the vibrant, articulate voice on her outgoing message to experience it. Instead of the politely passive wish that her caller "have a great day," she encourages that caller to take charge of the day's outcome, enthusiastically telling her, "*you* make it a great day." This is a prime example of Mrs. Walker's basic belief that the responsibility for an individual's success or failure lies solely with that individual.

"I feel that people choose to make detours in their lives. No one is responsible for my successes *but me*. No one is responsible for my failures *but me*. It doesn't matter who you are. We all start off on the same road. The detour you choose to make is your decision." The road taken by Mrs. Walker has been one of hard work, determination, enthusiasm, and innovation which has led her to become the successful and educated corporate executive, athlete, entrepreneur, and pillar of the community she is today.

After finishing her bachelor's degree in Business Marketing, Mrs. Walker began a successful career in marketing and management. Using her outstanding drive and leadership skills, she quickly worked her way up the corporate ranks to the executive level. She then returned to school to earn an MBA. Her volunteer marketing promotions and endeavors have included marketing and promoting the Atlanta Beat, Atlanta's team in the Women's United Soccer Association. She has also worked closely with the Atlanta Falcons, and is currently a member of the Atlanta Sports Council, which has been fundamental in drawing to Atlanta such major sporting events as the 1996 Summer Olympics, and Super Bowls XXVIII (1994) and XXXIV (2000). In addition, her sports involvement continues to involve her in major sports events including the XXXIX (2005) NFL Super Bowl in Jacksonville, Florida, the 2003 NCAA Women's Final Four in Atlanta, Georgia and the 2005 NCAA Women's Final Four in Indianapolis, Indiana. She is active in her local Chamber of Commerce and is also a member of the Atlanta Track Club and the WBCA-Women's Basketball Coaches Association.

Mrs. Walker runs marathons for local charities. When asked what inspired her to get involved in running for charity, she replies that she actually began training for marathons "On a dare. My dad once jokingly said that I couldn't run two miles. I ran two miles *that day*, and then he said, 'Ok, champ. What are you going do *next*?' I told him, 'I'm going to run a marathon.' He casually said 'Yeah, right: You just ran two miles, and now you're going to run twenty-six?" Mrs. Walker says that this comment inspired her to immediately join The Leukemia and Lymphoma Society's "Team In Training" ® program, which provided her with five months of marathon training in exchange for work in raising money to find a cure for these diseases. This was six years ago, and Mrs. Walker is still running.

Although it was family pressure, and especially her father's direct challenge, which prompted Mrs. Walker to become an athlete in the first place, the knowledge that she can make a difference in the lives of others is what inspires her today. "I run for children in the state of Georgia who have lymphoma or leukemia. So, I'm doing something for someone else. I'm making it to the finish line for them." Her next goal as an athlete is to work cycling, already a favorite hobby of hers, into her charitable athletic endeavors.

In addition to her accomplishments as a runner, Monique holds certifications in both kickboxing and personal training. She has used the training she received in earning these certificates to formulate her own exercise class, which she has dubbed "UltimateNRG." She describes it as "an awesome blend of kickboxing and boot camp-style aerobics." Mrs. Walker shares UltimateNRG with residents of battered womens' shelters throughout the Southeast. Her goal, she says, is to "get them moving, uplift their spirits, and increase their self-esteem." Mrs. Walker has also taught the class to property management companies, women organizations, schools in both Georgia and Florida, and churches throughout the southeast.

In addition to her dynamic career as a marketing executive, Monique travels throughout the Southeast hosting motivational seminars for women's retreats, college campuses, high schools, athletic centers, inner city youth centers, and churches. The crux of her message is that individuals can and should make the most out of whatever resources they are given in life. She credits her family with having instilled this idea in her at a very early age, and uses something many are familiar with—a child's weekly allowance—as an example.

"I remember that my dad would give us (Mrs. Walker and her older sister and younger brother) ten dollars for an allowance. Three dollars went to mom for food, and three dollars went to dad for room and board. We would put a dollar in the church (offering plate) on Sundays, and we had three dollars to spare. Every weekend we went somewhere as a family. At lunchtime, dad always bought lunch and a snack for every body. At around ten, my brother would want a treat. Dad would say "son, you can buy your treat with your three dollars." So, my brother never had any money. I would hold on to my three dollars, and at twelve o'clock, and then the treat that I had wanted at ten, my dad would include with my lunch. So, I always had money." Because she had learned to delay her gratification, she was able to receive the reward she'd wanted without losing any of her resources in the process.

Mrs. Walker credits her father, a construction worker and

avid sports fanatic himself, with instilling her with the raw material for success: "My dad has been athletic all his life. Every male in the family on my dad's side was athletic. If you were a Chandler and weren't athletic, no one knew you." Mrs. Walker says that it was the Chandler name, and not her own desire, which prompted her to join the cross-country and volleyball teams in high school. At the time, she didn't push herself to be active in the competitions, because they did not inspire her. Many would see that kind of pressure to live up to the family name as a negative. Most people would rebel against the pressure of the family name, and not get involved in sports ever again.

Then again, Mrs. Walker is not most people. She manages to see the best in every situation. She doesn't see the pressure to live up to the family name as a burden. She sees it instead as a challenge. "My dad always challenged me. I never understood why, because I was a little kid. Every time I presented something (that I wanted to do) to him, he would challenge me with it to see how far I could take it." She continues to take on her father's challenge, incorporating it into every aspect of her life.

Monique Chandler Walker's goal now is to inspire other women to challenge themselves in the same way her father has challenged her, and the way she has learned to challenge herself. Her motivational, uplifting seminars teach women everywhere how to do just that. Not only is she teaching women but takes her motivation to students as they prepare to take state exams throughout the Southeast. Her further commitment to youth is evident as she spearheaded a scholarship fund to assist students from her childhood community.

She would love nothing more than to show you how you, too, can "make it a great day."

Monique Chandler Walker lives in suburban Atlanta with her husband. She continues to work as a multi - task professional in sports, marketing, motivational speaking, group fitness instructor and as a collections director for a local corporation, and plans to run the Boston Marathon in the near future.

Monique is available for motivational speaking, assisting with sporting events and fitness seminars:

UltimateNRG Concepts

c/o Monique Chandler Walker

1000 Peachtree Industrial Blvd.

Suite 6-358

Suwanee, GA 30024

Bus: 678-634-2910

Email: ultimatenrgconcepts@yahoo.com

Printed in the United States
37751LVS00002B/4

9 780976 369882